INTRODUCING

NIGERIA

A to Z

ADISA BAKARE

AYISHA BELGORE

ENIOLA HARRISON

FARAFINA.LAGOS

Published in Nigeria in 2007 by
Farafina
An imprint of Kachifo Limited
25 Boyle Street
Onikan, Lagos Island
P. O. Box 72973
Victoria Island
Lagos, Nigeria
Tel: +234 1 2702372, 234 1 8162693
Mobile: +234 803 403 8974
Email: info@kachifo.com
www.kachifo.com

The rights of Adisa Bakare, Ayisha Belgore and Eniola Harrison to be identified as the authors of this work
have been asserted by them in accordance with the copyright laws.

A catalogue record for this book is available from the National Library of Nigeria.

ISBN 978-978-48012-4-9

All Photographs by George Osodi except
Pages 21 and 34 [from www.naijajams.com and www.africahit.com]

Typeface and Layout Design: Lanre Lawal, Kunle Ajose and Anne Imomoh
Text Typeface: Garrison Light Sans

This Farafina Educational Book Belongs To:

_____

_____

_____

ARTS & CRAFTS

The arts and craft of Nigeria differ from region to region. In the northern part of the country, people use clay, gourds and mud to create pottery and other utensils. In the south, people use cane to make chairs and tables. People also make baskets from palm branches and use metals like bronze and iron to make beautiful objects. There are many old objects that have been discovered that were made thousands of years ago. The Nok terracotta* heads, the sculpture in ivory and bronze castings from Ile-Ife, the metal utensils from Igbo-Ukwu, the leather-works from the north and the oldest boat ever found in Africa are just some of the few artefacts archaeologists have discovered.

GOURDS

These artefacts can be seen in Nigeria's many museums. Nigeria has many great artists who have created beautiful paintings and sculptures. Some of Nigeria's great artists are: Olowe of Ise-Ekiti; Bruce Onabrakpeya; Uche Okeke; Demas Nwoko; Yusuf Grillo; Erabor Emokpae; Abayomi Barber; Ben Enwonwu; Aina Onabolu; Ladi Kwali; Obiora Udechukwu; Gani Odutokun and Jerry Buhari.

*Terracotta is an unglazed brownish-orange substance made from a mixture of sand and clay used for pottery, statuettes and buildings.

Books

PROFESSOR WOLE SOYINKA

The literature of a community consists of the poems, stories and writings of that community. In the past, most of Nigeria's literature was oral. That means it was not written but passed on by mouth. Today, Nigeria has a great body of written literature that we can all read and enjoy. Nigeria has many great writers who write about the Nigerian way of life. Some of Nigeria's most famous books are *Things Fall Apart*, *The Lion and the Jewel* and *An African Night's Entertainment*.

SOME OF THE GREATEST NIGERIAN WRITERS ARE

Christopher Okigbo
Femi Osofisan
Wole Soyinka
Zainab Alkali
Nuhu Bamali
J. P. Clark
Mabel Segun
Flora Nwapa
D.O. Fagunwa
Gabriel Okara
Chinua Achebe
Seriki Aliyu Dan Sidi

BUILDINGS & MONUMENTS

Nigeria has a wide variety of interesting buildings. There is the National Arts Theatre which was built in 1977. It is considered to be one of Nigeria's most famous monuments.

The Gidan Makama Museum in Kano is another important monument. It was built in the 15th century by Emir Abdullahi Burja. Other impressive buildings include the Oba's palace in Benin, Old Residency in Calabar and the Mbari mud houses of Igbo land. Some of Nigeria's famous buildings and monuments include:

BUILDINGS & MONUMENTS

Chief Ogiamen's House, Benin City

This building is protected by the government because it is a fine example of Benin traditional architecture. It has an elaborate system of courtyards and altars. It is a chief's house and was probably built before the 1897 British expedition against Benin. The big fire that destroyed the city following the British invasion did not affect the building.

Gobirau Minaret, Katsina

This imposing minaret or tower, which was originally 120 metres tall and was built of mud and palm timbers, is all that remains of the mosque constructed before the holy wars of Usman Dan Fodio. Parts of the tower are thought to be at least 250 years old.

City Wall and Moat, Zaria

The Zaria City wall remains the best preserved among the cities of northern Nigeria. Although the rains of many wet seasons have battered down the tall mud walls in many northern cities, the walls of Zaria have still survived. The walls which surround the city are between 14 and 16 kilometers long and have eight gates.

Foot Bridge, Kaduna

This is an interesting example of indigenous engineering before the construction of roads and railways in Nigeria. The bridge was originally erected by Lord Lugard at Zungeru in 1904 and moved to the Kaduna Gardens in 1954.

CITIES

ABUJA AT NIGHT

A SECTION OF LAGOS ISLAND

The city of Lagos is one of the largest cities in Africa and the world. The Nigerian name for Lagos is Eko. It is Nigeria's main port. About 15 million people live and work in Lagos. Abuja is the capital of Nigeria. It is also the seat of Government. The President, the Chief Justice of Nigeria, members of the National Assembly and many important government officials all live and work in Abuja. Major cities in Nigeria are: Lagos; Enugu; Port Harcourt; Kano; Sokoto; Kaduna; Ibadan; Abuja; Maiduguri; Calabar and Onitsha.

CLIMATE

CLOUD FORMATIONS OVER SOUTHERN NIGERIA

Nigeria's climate is tropical. This means that the weather in the country is mainly hot. However, the temperature of most areas depends on the amount of rain that falls in that area. The climate of communities near the Atlantic Ocean, like Lagos State is very different from a state that is far away from the ocean like Kano.

Although Lagos is cooler than Kano, it is more humid than Kano because of the high moisture content in the air.

In Nigeria, it is usually coldest in the highland areas like Obudu and Jos. It is hottest and driest in the northern states, which share borders with the Sahara desert.

CLIMATE CHANGE

WE LIVE ON PLANET EARTH

The climate is the general weather of a place or region. Climate change refers to the changes in the earth's climate over time. Scientists believe that practices such as the cutting down of forests, burning of fossil fuel, and population growth are contributing to climate change.

Some effects of climate change include the desertification in northern Nigeria and the drying up of Lake Chad. Unusually heavy rainfall is causing some rivers to overflow, while evaporation is emptying others. Crops and livestock are being destroyed by drought.

Climate change and global warming are closely connected. Global warming refers to the fact that the weather is getting hotter all over the world. Scientists warn that if the present rate of global warming continues, it could lead to a rise in the level of the oceans. This rise will be enough to flood land in major coastal cities like Lagos, Calabar and Port Harcourt.

To slow down climate change, people need to reduce greenhouse gas emissions. The Greenhouse Effect is the rise in temperature that the earth experiences because certain gases in the atmosphere trap energy from the sun. As the Greenhouse Effect becomes stronger, it could lead to climate change. It is therefore important to do little things like turning off electricity when it is not in use, or planting trees like Wangari Maathai, the Kenyan Nobel Peace Prize winner.

CLOTHING

A FULANI GIRL

The way we dress is an important part of our culture. Nigerians dress differently according to the ethnic groups they belong to. In the east, Igbo women wear George wrappers and lace blouses. Yoruba men wear buba and sokoto, while the women wear iro, buba and gele.

In the north, Hausa men wear a babariga while the women usually use atampa (called ankara in the south) to make clothes.

However, the Fulani traditional attire is more elaborate. The men wear conical herdsman hats; in red, black, and natural colours; made of woven raffia and leather. They wear baggy leather or cloth trousers and wrap woven blankets with geometrical patterns around their bodies.

The women wear woven 'half tops' which stop above their navels with long skirts made of the same material.

The Fulani are also renowned for their elaborate art of body adornment. Men and women alike are fond of tattoos. They wear amulets (lohol) as both protective and decorative elements. Women wear heavy twisted gold earrings (dibi) and gold necklaces (caaka).

CLOTHING

YORUBA WOMEN

What we wear is influenced by the climate of the area we live in. Nigerians generally wear clothes made of light fabrics such as cotton, because the weather is usually hot. However, in countries where the weather gets very cold, such as Finland and Denmark, people will wear clothes made of thicker material to protect themselves from the cold. In Alaska, people wear clothes made of fur to keep themselves warm. If people in Nigeria wore clothes made of fur, they would be too hot.

CROPS

A NIGERIAN FARMER

Many Nigerians are farmers who grow different kinds of crops on their farms. Nigeria has a lot of arable land that is good for farming and so farmers are able to grow a variety of crops. Nigerian farmers grow two kinds of crops. The first are food crops, which we eat, such as yams, maize, beans and vegetables. The other kind of crops are cash crops, which we don't eat, such as cocoa, oil palm, rubber and cotton. Cash crops are sold to factories as raw materials to manufacture other products such as tyres, chocolate and cloth.

CULTURE

AN EFIK DANCER FROM CROSS RIVER

Every community has a culture. Culture is the way people live, their values and their beliefs. People who share the same culture, usually share the same languages. They eat the same food, dress the same way and share the same customs.

CULTURE

IGBO DANCERS FROM EBONYI

People who belong to the Igbo ethnic group share the same customs. They all speak the Igbo language, wear the same type of traditional clothes, and usually eat the same types of food. The world is full of people with different cultures. In Nigeria alone, there are about two hundred different ethnic groups.

CURRENCY

The money used in Nigeria is called the naira and kobo. Before the naira and kobo were introduced in 1973, Nigerians used the pound, shillings and pence just like the British. The symbol for the naira is ₦. 100 kobo make 1 Naira.

DEMOCRACY

THE NATIONAL ASSEMBLY COMPLEX IN ABUJA, CAPITAL CITY OF NIGERIA

Nigeria has a democratic government. Democracy means that we have the right to vote for the leaders of our choice. This means that we the citizens, have a say in what goes on in government. This type of government allows us to choose who we want to lead our country. In Nigeria, we choose our leaders every four years during the general elections. President Umaru Musa Yar'Adua is the current political leader of our country.

THE NIGERIAN ECONOMY

AN OIL RIG OFF THE COAST OF THE NIGER DELTA

A FARM-HAND

The Nigerian economy is based on what the country produces and sells. The goods and services a country sells to other countries are called exports. Nigeria is rich in mineral and agricultural resources like crude oil and natural gas, tin, columbite, limestone and palm oil. These resources are sold to other countries to generate income for the country.

Nigeria makes most of its money from exporting crude oil and natural gas. Crude oil is used to make petrol for our cars. From crude oil we also get diesel for generators and kerosene for cooking.

The Nigerian economy also depends on agricultural crops such as beans, rice, cassava, onions, tomatoes and yam. Crops that grow in the south such as plantain, cocoa, kola-nuts, cassava and oil palm are sold to people in the north, while the north sells cattle, vegetables and groundnuts to the south.

ETHNIC GROUPS

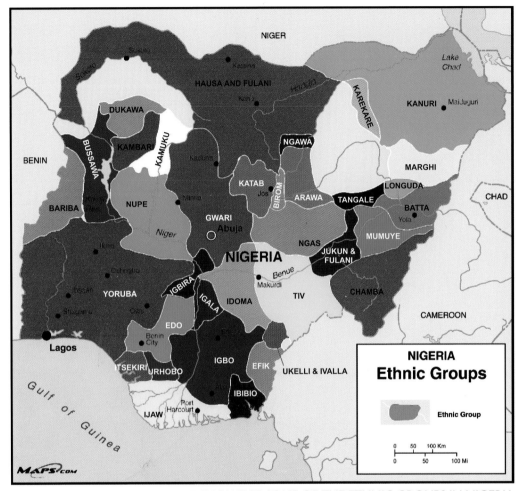

A MAP SHOWING SOME OF THE ETHNIC GROUPS IN NIGERIA

People who belong to the same ethnic group usually live in the same geographic area. They speak the same language. They usually eat the same type of food and wear the same clothes. There are over two hundred ethnic groups in Nigeria.

Although people belong to different ethnic groups, we must respect each other and try to understand how our differences influence the way we act or think. When we respect each other's differences we promote peace and our communities are better places.

FAMILY

Family life is a very important part of Nigerian culture. In Nigeria, we have the nuclear and extended family. The nuclear family consists of parents and children. The extended family includes grandparents, aunties, uncles and cousins. In some parts of Nigeria, it is the culture to have polygamous marriages. This means that a man can have more than one wife. However in many parts of Nigeria, a person usually has one spouse.

FESTIVALS

ARGUNGU FISHING FESTIVAL

Nigerians celebrate many local festivals that date far back in time. Festivals are celebrated for different reasons, from harvest to honouring ancestors.

The New Yam Festival (Iwa-ji or Iri-ji) is usually held in the beginning of August, at the end of the rainy season. During the festival, newly harvested yams are offered to gods and ancestors before people can start eating them. This is a traditional way of giving thanks for the harvest, honouring the ancestors and bringing the people together.

The Argungu Fishing Festival is a fishing competition held annually in Argungu, Sokoto State. During this festival, hundreds of fishermen rush into the Sokoto River and try to catch as many fish as possible. **The Durbar Festival** is held in most northern states of the country. During this festival, people ride and race horses.

In the south-west, there is the **Osun Osogbo Annual Festival** celebrating the Osun river goddess whose grove has been declared a UNESCO World Heritage site.

FILM

Nigerian movies depict the culture and way of life of the people and the country. Nigerian movies are popularly called 'home videos'. This is because they are shot with hand-held video cameras instead of 35mm cameras, which are used in more developed movie industries.

Nigeria's movie industry is huge and has been dubbed 'Nollywood'. Nollywood is the third largest film industry in the world, after Hollywood (the American film industry) and Bollywood (the Indian film industry).

Nigerian film producers now use modern equipment and the quality of the movies is improving.

Nigerian movies are enjoyed all over the world.

POSTERS OF NIGERIAN FILMS

FOLKTALES

Long before the invention of paper and ink, Nigerian people passed on their history and stories orally. Many of these stories and songs are still being passed on today. Here is a popular Nigerian folktale:

Once upon a time, there was famine in the animal kingdom. There was no food anywhere. All the animals were very hungry. There had been no rain for many months. The animals grew thinner and thinner. The only animals who remained fat and healthy were the birds. The tortoise asked the birds how they were so healthy. The birds told the tortoise that they had food in the sky.

One day there was a party in the sky and all the animals were invited. The birds carried the tortoise in between them and flew to the party in the sky. When the tortoise got to the party, he gave his name as "All of you."

When the hostess came out with the food, she said, 'This food is for "all of you."' The tortoise pounced on the food and ate up all of it without sharing with the other birds.

THE TORTOISE

The birds got very angry, especially as they had helped to bring the tortoise to the sky. They flew off in anger and left the tortoise at the party.

He was stuck in the sky, with no way to get back to earth. The tortoise had no choice but to jump down. He landed so hard that he broke his shell. That is why the tortoise has a broken shell.

FOLKSONGS

EGUNGUN MASQUERADE FROM OGUN

IGBO DANCER

A Yoruba Folksong:

Ìwé kíkọ́
la'ì sí ọkọ́
àti àdá
kò'ì pe ó, kò'ì pe ó.

Iṣẹ́ àgbè n'iṣẹ́ ilẹ̀ wa
eni kò s'iṣẹ́
á mà ja'lẹ̀.

English Translation:

Education
without the hoe
and the cutlass
is not complete, is not complete.

Farming is the work of our land
whoever does not work
will surely steal.

Igbo Song:

Akwukwo na ato uto.
O na ara ahu n' mmuta.
Onye nwere ntachi obi,
Oga amuta akwukwo,
O buru na nne ya na nna ya nwere ego,
O buru na nne ya na nna ya nwere ego.

English Translation:

Education is worthwhile.
It is hard to acquire.
But whoever perseveres
Can acquire education,
If the parents can afford it,
If the parents can afford it.

FOLKSONGS

WAR DANCERS FROM GOMBE

A Hausa Folksong:

Dan maliyo nawa
Chorus: Maliyo

Yaje ina ne?
Chorus: Maliyo

Ya je ilorin
Chorus: Maliyo

Bazai dawo ba?
Chorus: Maliyo

Sai a watan gobe
Chorus: Maliyo

Jibi da labari
Chorus: Maliyo

Chorus: Karkada mug an rawar ki
Aris. Aris. Aris. Ra warki Aris.

English Translation:

Where has he gone?
Chorus: Maliyo

He went to Ilorin
Chorus: Maliyo

Is he going to come back?
Chorus: Maliyo

Not till the coming month
Chorus: Maliyo

Tomorrow comes with news
Chorus: Maliyo

The day after even more news
Chorus: Maliyo

Chorus: Turn around and dance for us
Showing us your moves, Aris, Aris, Aris, your dance Aris.

FOOD

FOOD STAPLES

TOMATOES

MANGOES

Nigerians love good food. Garri is very popular in Nigeria and is made from cassava. Garri can be eaten with cold water, sugar and fried groundnuts or it can be eaten hot as eba with various types of soups. Nigerians also eat a lot of dishes made from yam such as boiled or fried yam and pounded yam. Rice is a main staple prepared in different forms such as jollof, fried rice or as a gruel. Nigerians eat many different dishes made from vegetables such as egusi, efo, afang, nsala and oha. Popular Nigerian snacks include chin chin, dankwa, gurudi, kokoro, kuli kuli, puff puff, kilishi and suya.

GOVERNMENT

PRESIDENT UMARU MUSA YAR'ADUA

THE NIGERIAN COAT OF ARMS

The government is a very important part of our everyday lives. Our government is made up of the group of men and women that we elect to lead our communities, our states and our country. As good citizens it is important for us to know how the government works.

Participating in government is important because it gives us the opportunity to influence what happens in our country.

HAIRSTYLES

BRAIDED HAIRSTYLE

Nigerian women are famous for their beautiful and intricate hairstyles. Nigerian women weave, thread and braid their hair in different shapes, sizes and styles. Some famous hairstyles are *Ghana weaving, Police cap, Sade Adu and Bob Marley.*

DANCERS FROM ONDO

HISTORY

SULTAN'S PALACE, SOKOTO

Nigeria has not always been the way we know it to be today. A long time ago, there was no country called Nigeria. Instead, the area we know today as Nigeria was made up of different kingdoms ruled by kings, obas and emirs. The African people of today are the descendants of great empires such as the Old Benin Empire, the Oyo Kingdom, the Sokoto Caliphate and the Kanem Borno Empire. These empires were well organized and many of them grew very rich from trading gold, ivory, salt and slaves with other kingdoms in Africa, Europe and the Middle East.

HOLIDAY

Nigerians celebrate several national or public holidays. There are the Christian holidays of Easter and Christmas, the Muslim holidays of Eid El Fitr and Eid El Kabir, and national holidays such as Independence Day and Democracy Day.

May Day	May 1st
Children's Day	May 27th
Democracy Day	May 29th
Independence Day	October 1st
Christmas	December 25th
Easter*	——
Eid-el Fitr*	——
Eid-el Kabir*	——

AMUSEMENT PARK IN NORTHERN NIGERIA

*The dates for these holidays, unlike others, depend on the movements of the moon around the earth and are therefore not fixed.

28

INDUSTRY

AN INDUSTRIAL AREA IN LAGOS

Nigerian industries manufacture a wide range of products. The Nigerian textile industry produces beautiful fabrics such as ankara and adire. Nigerian manufacturers also produce hair and beauty products such as soap and lotion. Companies such as the Nigerian Bottling Company and Nigerian Breweries produce soft drinks and beer. Nigerian industries manufacture food products such as cereals, pasta, rice, juice, milk, biscuits, sweets and sugar. Nigerian farmers sell frozen livestock such as chicken, turkey, fish and other seafood. The music industry is also developing fast with Nigerian artists such as Tuface Idibia, Femi Kuti and P-Square gaining acclaim and recognition all over the world. Tuface won the MTV Europe Awards for Best African Act in 2005.

JOBS

There are many meaningful ways of making a living in Nigeria. People go to university to learn how to become doctors, lawyers, engineers, architects, teachers, bankers, writers and artists. Other people are farmers, fishermen, miners or loggers, depending on the areas they live in. Most people who live around the riverine areas are fishermen and Nigerians who live in or around the rainforests, are usually farmers or loggers.

A SUGAR CANE FARMER

NIGERIANS AT WORK

KOLA NUT

The kola nut is known throughout Nigeria. It has been described as the national crop of Nigeria. The Yorubas of the south-west grow it, the Hausas of the north eat it and the Igbos of the south-east revere it.

LANGUAGE

All cultures have their own languages. A language is a way of communicating. Language is one of the most important aspects of culture because it is one of the first things we learn. There are over 200 languages spoken in Nigeria. Some of them are Hausa, Igbo, Yoruba, Itsekiri, Efik, Ijaw, Fulani and Ibibio. The official language of Nigeria is English. Many Nigerians also speak pidgin English which is a form of English. Language binds us to our communities and it is usually easy to identify a person's culture by the language they speak. For example, you know someone is Igbo or has affiliations with the Igbo when you hear them speak the Igbo language.

A YOUNG NIGERIAN COMMUNICATING BY TELEPHONE

MOUNTAINS & HIGHLANDS

IDANRE HILLS, ONDO

From the Middle Belt towards northern Nigeria exist the highlands of Nigeria. Nigeria's northern highlands include the Adamawa and Jos plateaux. A plateau is a highland with a flat top.

There are also highlands on the eastern border of Nigeria such as the Mandara Mountains, the Shebeshi Mountains, the Alantika Mountains and the Mambila Mountains.

Other highland areas of Nigeria include the Obudu plateau and the Udi and Oban Hills. These highlands have a cooler climate than other parts of Nigeria. This is because the higher you go, the cooler it becomes. Because the climate of places like Obudu and Jos is cooler, farmers are able to grow certain crops that cannot grow in other parts of Nigeria. In Jos, gardeners now grow roses and strawberries for export to other parts of the world.

Nigeria's highlands are also very rich in natural resources such as tin and coal and even gold. The highest point in Nigeria is the Chappal Wadi Mountain in Taraba State.

Music

Nigeria has a rich music culture. Nigerian music is loved and appreciated all over the world. There are different styles of music played in Nigeria. There is highlife, afro-beat, afro-jazz, hiphop, rhythm & blues, juju and fuji music. Nigeria has many great musicians who are famous around the world. One of Nigeria's most famous musicians was Fela Anikulapo-Kuti who perfected the afro-beat style of music. Ayo Bankole was a great Nigerian composer. He wrote beautiful music that we still enjoy today. Other great Nigerian musicians are King Sunny Ade, Chief Osita Osadebe, Naram Mada, Na Mangi, Dan Maraya-Jos, I. K. Dairo, Mamman Shaata, Dan Kwairo, Onyeka Onwenu and Comfort Omoge. Today, the Nigerian music industry is progressing from producing music which is mostly enjoyed by Nigerians and Africans to more contemporary music such as hip hop and rhythm & blues which can be enjoyed by everyone all over the world.

Young musicians like Asa, Dare Art Alade, D'banj, P-Square, Styl-Plus, Weird MC and Sound Sultan are taking Nigerian music international.

FELA KUTI

TUFACE IDIBIA

NATIONAL SYMBOLS

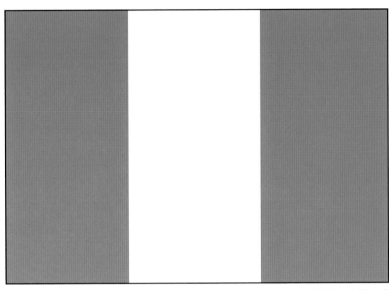

THE NIGERIAN FLAG

This is the Nigerian Flag. It is a symbol of national unity. The green parts of the flag represent Nigeria's soil which is rich and good for planting all types of crops. The white part of the flag represents peace.

The Nigerian National Anthem

Arise, O compatriots, Nigeria's call obey
To serve our fatherland
With love and strength and faith
The labour of our heroes past
Shall never be in vain
To serve with heart and might
One nation bound in freedom, peace and unity.

Oh God of creation, direct our noble cause
Guide our leaders right
Help our youth the truth to know
In love and honesty to grow
And living just and true
Great lofty heights attain
To build a nation where peace and justice
shall reign.

The National Pledge

I pledge to Nigeria my country
To be faithful, loyal and honest
To serve Nigeria with all my strength
To defend her unity
And uphold her honour and glory
So help me God.

NATIONAL SYMBOLS

THE NIGERIAN COAT OF ARMS

The Coat of Arms of Nigeria has a black shield with two white stripes that come together, like the letter Y. The Y-shape represents the two main rivers of Nigeria, the Niger and Benue rivers. The black shield represents Nigeria's good soil. The two horses on each side represent dignity. The eagle represents strength. The green and white bands on the top of the shield represent the rich agricultural land of the country. The flower in the grass is the crocus. It is Nigeria's national flower.

OIL &GAS

OIL TANK FARM IN BONNY

    The main export of Nigeria is crude oil. Nigeria produces two million barrels of crude oil every day and is currently the 5th largest producer of crude oil in the world. Crude oil is used to make petrol for cars. From crude oil we also get diesel for generators and kerosene for cooking. Nigeria also sells this crude oil to other countries. Natural gas, which can be found in huge quantities in Nigeria, is another main export of the country. Although Nigeria is famous for its crude oil production, Nigeria has more gas reserves than it does crude oil.

PEOPLE

IGBO WOMEN

FULANI BOY

YORUBA WOMAN

Nigeria is a very rich and diverse country. There are over 250 different ethnic groups and over 200 languages and dialects spoken in Nigeria. The Igbo people live in the south-east, the Yoruba live in the south-west and the Hausa live in the north. Other ethnic groups in Nigeria include Edo, Jukun, Igala, Igbira, Efik, Idoma, Fulani, Kanuri, Tiv, Ibibio, Itsekiri, Ijaw and Nupe.

POPULATION

OSHODI, A BUS STOP AND MARKET IN LAGOS

Nigeria has a population of over 130 million people. Population refers to a collection of people living in a geographic area. All Nigerians who live in the country belong to the country's population. Nigeria has the largest population in Africa.

R AIN

RAIN IN PORT HARCOURT

Rainfall is very important for the growth of vegetation. In the south of Nigeria, it rains more frequently than in the north. That is why we have lush vegetation in southern Nigeria and drier vegetation in the north.

RELIGION

THE ANGLICAN CATHEDRAL CHURCH, LAGOS

CENTRAL MOSQUE, ABUJA

In Nigeria, we have people who are Muslims, Christians, and also others who practice traditional religions. It is very important to respect people's religion. Sometimes people's religion affects their culture. For example, the culture and tradition of Yoruba Muslims are a bit different from that of Yoruba Christians.

Nigeria is a country with different people, which means we must learn to be tolerant. Being tolerant means not only understanding that everyone is different, but also accepting and celebrating their differences.

RESOURCES

LIQUEFIED NATURAL GAS PLANT, BONNY

Resources are the things such as land, minerals and natural energy that exist in a country and can be used to increase its wealth. Some resources are man-made while others are natural. Nigeria has many natural resources. Examples of these are mineral resources such as natural gas, petroleum, tin and iron.

There are agricultural resources such as yam, maize, cocoa, oil palm, groundnut, rubber and cotton. These are crops that can be used to make beverages, confectionery, tyres, clothes and chocolates.

RIVERS & LAKES

FIVE COWRIE CREEK, LAGOS

Nigeria has many rivers, which contain fish and other seafood. They also provide water for many people. Nigeria's largest river is the Niger, which flows from Guinea into north-western Nigeria and empties into the Atlantic Ocean through the Niger delta. Nigeria's other major river is the Benue, which flows into eastern Nigeria from Cameroun. There are other rivers in Nigeria such as Ogun, Cross, Hadejia, Osun, Imo, Anambra, Sokoto and Osse.

River Niger is the third largest river in Africa as well as the largest river in West Africa. River Niger begins in the Futa Jalon Hills and runs through Guinea, Mali, Niger Republic and Nigeria. River Niger is very important because it provides food, drinking water and water for farming for the people who live around the river. It also provides electricity for many people.

Nigeria's other major river, River Benue, rises in northern Cameroun and flows into Nigeria through Yola in Adamawa State and Makurdi in Benue State. The Benue River is an important transportation route. It joins the River Niger at the famous confluence in Lokoja.

RIVERS & LAKES

OGUTA LAKE, IMO

Nigeria is home to part of Lake Chad. A lake is a large area of fresh or salt water surrounded by land. Lake Chad is surrounded by Nigeria, the Niger Republic, the Chad Republic and Cameroon. Lake Chad used to be one of Africa's largest lakes. However, the climate's increasing heat, as well as human demand for water, has reduced the size of the lake.

Recent satellite photographs of Lake Chad show that the lake is almost no longer in Nigeria. Another famous lake in Nigeria is the Kainji lake. It is a man-made lake that was created in the 1960s when the Kainji Dam was built on the River Niger to produce electricity for the country.

SCHOOLS

ST GREGORY'S COLLEGE, LAGOS

In Nigeria, children either go to public or private schools. The public schools are run by the government and are tuition-free until the university level. Individuals or organisations own private schools. After secondary school, many Nigerian students either move on to universities or polytechnics. There are **66** universities and **39** polytechnics in the country.

SPORTS

NATIONAL STADIUM, ABUJA

Sports has always been an important part of Nigerian life. Football is the most popular sport in Nigeria. Nigeria's national team, the Super Eagles have won the African Nations Championship Cup twice. Nigeria's under-23 football team won the Olympic gold medal in 1996. Nigeria's national female football team the Super Falcons have won the African Women's Championship a record four times.

Other sports at which Nigerians excel include wrestling, boxing, table-tennis, weight-lifting and athletics. Nigeria has won medals in these sports at the Olympic Games.

STATE CAPITALS

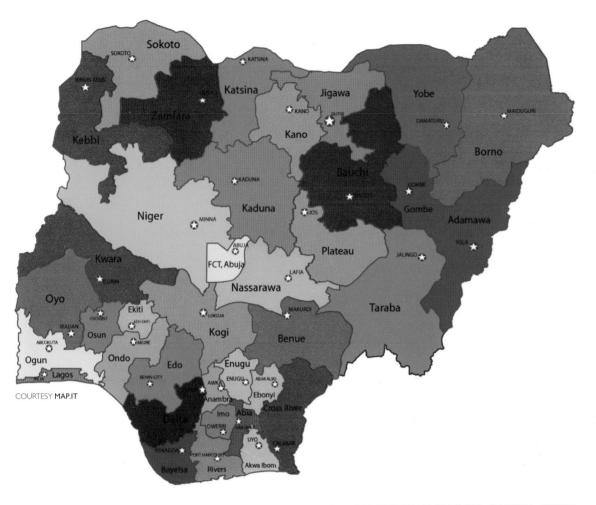

NIGERIAN STATES AND THEIR CAPITAL CITIES

Abia	Umuahia
Adamawa	Yola
Akwa Ibom	Uyo
Anambra	Awka
Bauchi	Bauchi
Bayelsa	Yenagoa
Benue	Makurdi
Borno	Maiduguri
Cross River	Calabar
Delta	Asaba
Ebonyi	Abakaliki
Edo	Benin City
Ekiti	Ado-Ekiti
Enugu	Enugu
Gombe	Gombe
Imo	Owerri
Jigawa	Dutse
Kaduna	Kaduna
Kano	Kano
Katsina	Katsina
Kebbi	Birnin-Kebbi
Kogi	Lokoja
Lagos	Ikeja
Nasarawa	Lafia
Niger	Minna
Ogun	Abeokuta
Ondo	Akure
Osun	Oshogbo
Oyo	Ibadan
Plateau	Jos
Rivers	Port Harcourt
Sokoto	Sokoto
Taraba	Jalingo
Yobe	Damaturu
Zamfara	Gusau

Here are the Nigerian states and their capitals. There are thirty-six states in total. The capital city of Nigeria is Abuja, in the Federal Capital Territory, Abuja.

TOURIST ATTRACTIONS

OBUDU CATTLE RANCH, CROSS RIVER

Nigeria is a rich and diverse country with interesting sights and sounds. Nigeria has kilometres of sandy beaches in the south, hills and caves in the southern rainforests, teeming waterfalls, quiet lakes, and a wide and diverse wildlife.

Nigeria is also home to a number of national parks where a wide variety of plant and animal life is protected and preserved. Some of the more famous national parks are Obudu Cattle Ranch, Yankari National Park, Kanji Lake National Park and Old Oyo National Park.

TOURIST ATTRACTIONS

EYO FESTIVAL

Nigeria also has many cultural attractions such as the **Osun Oshogbo** and **Eyo Festivals** in the south-west, the **Durbar Festival** in the north and the **New Yam Festival** in the south-east.

TRANSPORTATION

ONITSHA BRIDGE

People in Nigeria move from one place to another using different means. In the cities, people drive cars or use the public transportation system of buses. In Lagos, taxis are painted yellow with two black stripes. The colour of a taxi depends on the state you are in. People also use motorbikes, canoes and boats to get around depending on where they live. People who live in the villages may use bicycles to get from one place to another.

VEGETATION

AN AERIAL VIEW OF THE NIGER DELTA

The vegetation of an area refers to the different types of plants, grasses and trees that grow in that particular area. The vegetation in Nigeria differs depending on the region. Because the weather in Nigeria is hot, the amount of water in an area determines the type of vegetation in that area. Some types of vegetation found in Nigeria include the desert, the sahel savannah and the guinea savannah, which can mainly be found toward the northern areas of the country. Other types of vegetation found in Nigeria include the mangrove swamps and rainforest, which are mainly found in the southern and coastal areas of the country.

WILDLIFE

ELEPHANTS AT THE YANKARI GAME RESERVE

Most wild animals in Nigeria no longer roam free. They now live in game reserves where they have enough food and are protected from poachers. Poachers hunt animals for their valuable skin, horns and meat. Animals such as elephants, leopards, lions, zebras and gorillas now live in wildlife parks like the Yankari Game Reserve and the Cross River National Park. The Cross River National Park is home to the only remaining Cross River Gorillas in the world. There are only two hundred of these beautiful animals left in the world.

XYLOPHONE

A WOODEN XYLOPHONE

The xylophone is a popular musical instrument in Nigeria. Xylophones are made of wooden bars of different lengths. Each bar is tuned to a specific note on the musical scale. The instrument is played by striking the wooden bars with two wooden mallets. The xylophone is used by many dance troupes from different parts of Nigeria during their performances.

YAMS

YAM TUBERS

Yams are one of the most important food staples in Nigeria. They are a major part of the Nigerian diet. Yam can be eaten and cooked in so many different ways. It can be eaten boiled or roasted. It can be fried as dundun or pounded as iyan and nni jii. Yam flour can also be eaten as amala or lafun. Yams are also a symbol of wealth in certain parts of the country.

The New Yam Festival, celebrated by the Igbo is the time when the old yams of the previous year are thrown away to make way for new harvest.

ZUMA ROCK

ZUMA ROCK

Zuma is a huge rock formation on the road to Abuja. Towering across the skyline, Zuma Rock is sometimes called the *Gateway to Abuja*.